RECIPES AND PHOTOGRAPHS
SANDRA MAHUT

Unicorn Food

MURDOCH BOOKS
SYDNEY · LONDON

Table of contents

Recipes for happiness

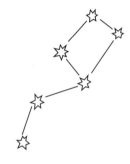

THE PRINCIPLE

We are fascinated by the unicorn – a fantastic, fabulous being! When its colourful universe lands on our plate, we smile. The aim is to eat a rainbow, but a healthy one, thanks to recipes that are both balanced and colourful, that will delight the eyes as well as the taste buds.

We are often wary of conventional food colourings (too many chemicals, harmful to health...). 'Natural' food colourings allow you to decorate and give originality to your creations just as well as conventional food colourings, but safely. No artificial food colourings are used in this book: they are all plant-based.

The sweet and savoury recipes offered here are equally spectacular, to eat as well as look at.

NATURAL FOOD COLOURINGS

Many of the products we use every day have powerful colouring properties – colours that can be extracted by boiling, blending and so on.

This is the case with spinach leaves, beetroot or carrot juice, but also spices, for example turmeric and paprika.

To save time, you can use natural powdered food colourings found in specialty cake-decorating shops or on the internet.

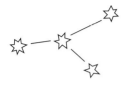

MAKING PRETTY COLOURS

Blue: red cabbage juice + lemon; curaçao or natural powdered blue food colouring (blue spirulina, acai or klamath); powdered food colouring for cake decorating derived from phycocyanin (a blue pigment contained in a micro algae derived from spirulina)

Purple: blueberry juice; beetroot; acai powder

Mauve: red cabbage juice

Yellow: curry powder; turmeric; bee pollen grains ground to a powder

Orange-yellow: turmeric

Pink/Red: raspberry juice (or the juice of another berry); beetroot juice; roselle (hibiscus) juice; achiote seeds, infused and mixed with almond milk or fromage frais

Green: green spirulina; spinach juice; matcha; barley grass juice powder

Orange: carrot juice; sea buckthorn berry juice; paprika

Mermaid toast

Preparation time: 5 minutes

Makes 4 pieces of toast

4 slices sandwich bread or square
crispbreads
200 g cream cheese
2–3 drops each of natural blue,
green and pink food colouring
Raspberry or blackcurrant coulis
1 pinch blue and green spirulina
1 pinch edible glitter

Toast the bread.

Keep half the cream cheese plain and divide the
rest into three, using the food colouring to create
three different colours of cream cheese.

Spread a layer of plain cream cheese on each toast,
top with a layer of coloured cream cheese, then
a few drops of rasberry or blackcurrant coulis or
sprinkle with blue or green spirulina. Spread with
a palette knife. Sprinkle with glitter and serve
immediately!

*To make them even more fairytale-like, you can
add dragon fruit slices cut into flower or star shapes
using a cookie cutter, or cucumber shapes coloured
with a drop of blackcurrant coulis.*

SAVOURY

Unicorn dips

Preparation time: 25 minutes

Serves 4

Hummus
1 tablespoon tahini (white sesame paste)
500 g tinned chickpeas
2 garlic cloves
Juice of 1 lemon
50 ml olive oil
2 teaspoons salt
300 g beetroot, cooked sous vide
1 teaspoon natural blue powdered food colouring or powdered blue spirulina

Sesame guacamole
2 ripe avocados
2 tablespoons olive oil
Lemon juice
Salt and pepper
1 pinch green spirulina

Fresh vegetables and sesame seeds for decoration

Making the hummus
Dilute the tahini in 50 ml hot water. Drain the chickpeas. Cut the garlic cloves in half. Blend together the tahini, chickpeas, garlic and olive oil in a food processor until you have a very smooth purée. Add salt to taste. Divide the mixture into two portions. Set aside in the refrigerator.

For the pink hummus, blend the cooked beetroot and mix into one portion of the mixture.

For the blue hummus, mix the natural blue food colouring into the other portion, then place a drop of liquid blue food colouring in the middle for a guaranteed 'mermaid' effect.

Decorate with stars of carrot, cucumber or pink radish, cut out with a cookie cutter.

Making the guacamole
Mash all the ingredients or blend in a food processor. Add a little extra olive oil or water to make the guacamole smooth. Check for seasoning.

Top with white sesame seeds and some cucumber stars.

Serve with grissini (breadsticks) for dipping.

Rainbow veggie sandwich

Preparation time: 20 minutes

Makes 2 sandwiches

4 crispbreads or slices of toasted
seeded bread
2 carrots
1 raw beetroot
2 tablespoons olive oil
2 pinches pink Himalayan salt
1 tomato
1 avocado
½ cucumber
½ mango
½ iceberg lettuce
50 g red cabbage
A few pink radishes
2 tablespoons grated surimi
1 tablespoon mayonnaise with
1 drop natural pink food colouring
50 g cream cheese
natural blue food colouring or blue
spirulina

Peel and cut the carrots and raw beetroot into matchsticks, then place them in separate small bowls. Drizzle them with a little olive oil and add a pinch of pink salt. Let them marinate.

Thinly slice the tomato, avocado, cucumber, mango, iceberg lettuce, red cabbage and radishes. Mix the grated surimi in a bowl with the pink mayonnaise.

Place 2 slices of bread or crispbread on a plate, spread with a little cream cheese, add a little spirulina or natural food colouring and spread again with the spatula, as for the mermaid toast. Lay on slices of tomato, cucumber, avocado, iceberg lettuce and mango, then the carrot matchsticks, then a layer of pink mayonnaise, then the red cabbage, beetroot matchsticks and radish slices.

Top each sandwich with a slice of bread spread with cream cheese in the same way as the first slice. Wrap the sandwiches tightly in plastic wrap.

Keep in the refrigerator for 1 to 2 hours.

Cut each sandwich in two at serving time.

Unicorn rice paper rolls

Preparation time: 15 minutes

Makes 6 small rice paper rolls

½ packet bean thread vermicelli
1–2 drops natural blue food colouring or blue spirulina
1 carrot
1 cucumber
½ red cabbage
A few pink radishes
½ avocado
6 rice paper wrappers
A few green lettuce leaves
A few black and white sesame seeds
½ mango for decoration

Lemon coconut tahini sauce
1 tablespoon tahini
1 tablespoon sesame oil
Juice of ½ lime
1 tablespoon coconut cream
1 teaspoon light soy sauce
1 drop natural blue food colouring

Cook the vermicelli according to the instructions on the packet, adding a little blue food colouring to the cooking water. Once the vermicelli is coloured, set aside in a bowl of cold water. Cut the carrot and half the cucumber into thin matchsticks. Thinly slice the red cabbage. Slice the radishes into rounds and thinly slice the avocado.

Moisten a sheet of rice paper and place it on a slightly damp, clean tea towel. Cut off the top edge of the wrapper (to give a straight side for an open-ended roll). Arrange the lettuce leaves and vegetables in the middle, starting with the ingredients that will show through. Wrap up the roll, using your fingertips to tightly close the lower part.

Place the rolls in the refrigerator. At serving time, sprinkle with black and white sesame seeds, then decorate with stars cut out of the mango or the rest of the cucumber.

Blend the sauce ingredients, except the food colouring, in a food processor. Add the drop of blue food colouring and swirl once with the tip of a knife to make a pretty spiral, then sprinkle with a few sesame seeds. Serve the rolls with the sauce.

Unicorn maki rolls

Preparation time: 20 minutes – Cooking time: 50 minutes – Resting time: 1 night

Makes about 10 makis (two long rolls)

1 small bamboo mat
½ large-leafed green lettuce
2 sticks surimi
1 cucumber
1 avocado
Wasabi and sesame seeds
Soy sauce seasoned with a drop
of sesame oil and a few black and
white sesame seeds

Vinegared rice
150 g short-grain sushi rice
150 ml water
2 to 3 tablespoons rice vinegar
1 teaspoon fine salt
1 tablespoon caster sugar
Natural pink, blue, yellow and
purple food colouring

Making the vinegared rice
Cook the rice according to the instructions on the packet. Once cooked, remove the lid of the saucepan and let the rice rest for 10 minutes.

Heat the vinegar, salt and sugar together in a saucepan and mix to dissolve the sugar and salt, without bringing to the boil. Allow to cool.

Divide the vinegar mixture between four bowls, adding drops of food colouring to each bowl.

Place the rice in a large mixing bowl to cool, then divide it between the bowls of vinegar to make blue, pink, purple and yellow rice.

Making the maki rolls
Wash and dry the lettuce leaves and cut them into thick, rectangular bands. Place the lettuce bands on the bamboo mat, then lay a line of each coloured rice, about ½ cm thick, to make a sort of rainbow. Place a strip of surimi, avocado and cucumber on top. Roll the rice onto itself with the help of the mat, rolling tightly so it is firm. Repeat the process for the second roll.

Place the rolls in the refrigerator overnight.
The next day, cut them into sections 3 cm wide.
Serve immediately with wasabi and sesame seeds, with the soy and sesame sauce on the side.

Veggie noodle bowl

Preparation time: 40 minutes – Cooking time: 40 minutes – Resting time: 10 minutes

Makes 2 bowls

100 g rice vermicelli
2 drops natural blue liquid food colouring
2 drops natural purple or fuchsia pink food colouring
1 avocado
½ dragon fruit
5 pink radishes
½ red beetroot
½ cucumber
Black and white sesame seeds
A few blue edible flowers (pansy or borage)

Sauce
1 tablespoon tahini
1 teaspoon white miso
2 tablespoons lemon juice
1 tablespoon soy sauce
1 pinch ground ginger
1 tablespoon sesame oil
1 tablespoon coconut milk
1 tablespoon hot water

Make the sauce by mixing all of the ingredients together.

Cook the vermicelli according to the instructions on the packets in two saucepans, one with blue food colouring, the other with pink food colouring. Once the vermicelli is coloured, set aside in bowls of cold water.

Drain and arrange the two coloured noodles in two bowls, then add thinly sliced avocado and dragon fruit, the radishes cut into rounds, and the raw beetroot and cucumber cut into stars with a cookie cutter. Sprinkle with black and white sesame seeds and edible flowers.

Serve with the sauce poured over the top and mix well before enjoying.

You can of course add other kinds of fruit or vegetables to this bowl: halved strawberries, rocket, yellow capsicum (bell pepper), spring onion, etc.

Croque-unicorn

Preparation time: 10 minutes – Cooking time: 5 minutes

Makes 4 croque-unicorns

150 g grated mozzarella cheese
100 g grated gruyère cheese
Natural food colouring (4 different colours)
8 slices white sandwich bread
20 g butter
120 g mortadella

Mix the cheeses together and divide between four bowls. Add a few drops of each food colouring and mix to colour evenly.

Butter the eight slices of bread on both sides.

Arrange the four coloured cheeses on four of the slices of bread in side-by-side strips. Add a slice of mortadella, cover with another layer of coloured cheese strips and top with another slice of bread.

Cook the croque-unicorns, two at a time,
in a sandwich toaster for 5 minutes at 180°C,
or in the oven for 5 minutes at 200°C.

Celestial swirl soup

Preparation time: 10 minutes – Cooking time: 30 to 40 minutes

Serves 4

400 g purple carrots
150 g red cabbage
1 red onion
20 g salted butter
800 ml vegetable stock
Salt and pepper
200 ml pouring cream
2 pinches natural blue powdered food colouring (or blue spirulina)
White sesame seeds
Edible blue flowers (such as borage)

Wash and peel the carrots and red cabbage and cut them into chunks. Finely chop the red onion. Melt the butter in a flameproof casserole dish and add the onion. Sweat the onion and add the carrots and red cabbage. Pour in the stock and season with salt and pepper. Cover and cook for about 30–40 minutes.

Blend well in a food processor, adding a little pouring cream.

When serving in bowls, drizzle over some pouring cream and add some blue food colouring. Sprinkle with white sesame seeds and add a few flowers.

Serve immediately.

You can also add some orange or lemon zest.

Rainbow pancakes

Preparation time: 10 minutes – Cooking time: 15 to 20 minutes – Resting time: 30 minutes

Makes 12 pancakes

250 g plain (all-purpose) flour
1 pinch fine salt
50 g golden caster sugar
1 sachet (7.5 g) vanilla sugar
or 1 teaspoon liquid vanilla extract
10 g baking powder
2 organic eggs
50 ml sunflower or grapeseed oil
150 ml full-cream milk
Natural food colouring (green, blue, yellow and pink)
60 g white chocolate melts
Coloured decorations for sprinkling
Coconut flakes

Mix together the flour, salt, sugar, vanilla sugar (or extract) and baking powder in a mixing bowl. Add the eggs one at a time, whisking with a fork. Add the oil and whisk again. Pour in the milk and whisk until the batter is quite smooth.

Divide the batter between three or four bowls (depending on the number of colours), add a little natural food colouring to each, mix well and let the batter stand at room temperature for 30 minutes.

Pour a small ladleful of batter into a hot, greased frying pan, turning over each pancake when bubbles appear. Stack the cooked pancakes on a plate. Melt the white chocolate in a double boiler. Pour the melted white chocolate over the pancakes, decorate and sprinkle with coconut flakes.

Blueberry galaxy cupcakes

Preparation time: 1 hour – Cooking time: 25 minutes – Resting time: 1 hour

Makes 6 to 7 cupcakes

130 g plain (all-purpose) flour
80 g sugar
1 teaspoon baking powder
1 pinch salt
1 egg
70 ml milk
30 ml sunflower oil
100 g blueberries
Decorations: silver, blue, star-shaped, etc.

Frosting
25 g unsalted butter, softened
110 g cream cheese
50 g icing sugar
50 g mascarpone cheese
Natural food colouring (dark blue, light blue and purple)

Preheat the oven to 180°C.

Mix together the flour, sugar, baking powder and salt in a large mixing bowl.

Beat the egg in another mixing bowl, then add the milk and oil. Incorporate the dry mixture into the wet mixture, then add the blueberries and mix very gently so you don't damage them. Divide the batter between paper cupcake cases.

Bake for 20 minutes. Remove from the oven and let the cupcakes cool on a rack for 30 minutes before decorating them.

Frosting & decoration
Beat the softened butter with the cream cheese in a mixing bowl with an electric beater. Make sure it is quite smooth, then add the icing sugar and mascarpone. Beat the mixture for a few minutes until it is very smooth.

Divide this mixture between three bowls. Add a few drops of food colouring to each bowl. Mix each colour separately so they are quite different.

Fill one piping bag with the three coloured frostings. Place the bag in the refrigerator for 30 minutes. Pipe frosting onto each cupcake, pressing gently and making circles. Decorate the cupcakes.

The cupcakes will keep for 2 days in the refrigerator in an airtight container.

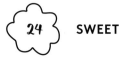

Rainbow cupcakes

Preparation time: 1 hour – Cooking time: 25 minutes – Resting time: 1 hour

Makes 6 cupcakes

85 g softened butter
100 g caster sugar
1 egg
130 g plain (all-purpose) flour
1 teaspoon vanilla liquid or powder
1 teaspoon baking powder
1 pinch salt
90 ml milk
50 g strawberries
Sugar decorations, paper unicorns

Frosting
25 g butter
110 g cream cheese
50 g icing sugar
50 g mascarpone cheese
A few drops natural food colouring
(blue, pink, green, yellow and
purple)
A little candy floss to decorate

Preheat the oven to 180°C.

Beat the butter with the sugar in a mixing bowl, then add the egg.

In another mixing bowl, mix together the flour, vanilla, baking powder and salt, then stir in half of this dry mixture into the wet mixture. Add half the milk and beat. Add the other half of the dry mixture and milk and beat until the batter is smooth and well combined.

Fill six paper cupcake cases three quarters full and bake for 20–25 minutes. Remove from the oven and allow to cool for 30 minutes before decorating.

Once they have cooled, remove a teaspoon of cake from the middle and push half a strawberry into the hole (or a whole strawberry if it is small).

Frosting & decoration
Follow the instructions for making the frosting on page 24.

Divide this mixture between five bowls, and add a few drops of blue, pink, purple, yellow and green food colouring to each bowl. Mix in each colour well with a soft spatula. Fill the one piping bag with all the frosting colours.

Once the cupcakes have cooled, make rainbows with the multicoloured frosting in the piping bag. Top with a piece of candy floss and decorate with a paper unicorn, or a horn made from fondant icing.

SWEET

Cosmic donuts

Preparation time: 30 min – Cooking time: 20 minutes – Resting time: 1 hour 30 mins + 1 hour drying time

Makes 6 donuts

3 g fresh yeast
90 ml lukewarm water (20°C)
140 g plain (all-purpose) flour

1 tablespoon milk
20 g fresh yeast, extra
30 g sugar
125 g plain (all-purpose) flour
4 egg yolks
5 g salt
30 g softened butter
1 litre oil for deep frying
Edible silver glitter, metallic cachous, etc.

Icing

1 egg white
250 g icing sugar
1 squeeze lemon juice
Natural blue food colouring

Crumble the yeast, pour over the lukewarm water to dissolve it, add the flour and mix together. Form into a ball, and let it rise in a warm but turned-off oven for 1 hour.

Place this starter in a mixing bowl or the bowl of a stand mixer. Work the dough with your fists or use the kneading setting for 3 minutes, then add the milk while continuing to knead.

Stir in the extra crumbled yeast, then sugar, flour, egg yolks and salt. Work the dough for 3 minutes. It should be very smooth. Add the softened butter.

Shape into a ball and cover with plastic wrap. Let it rise for 1 hour. The dough should double in volume.

Make identical portions of dough (30–40 g balls). Make a hole in the middle with your finger, then widen the hole to give it a donut shape.

Place the donuts on a baking tray lined with baking paper and let them rise for at least 30 minutes at room temperature. Deep fry them in the oil at 180°C for 3 minutes on each side. Drain and place on paper towels.

Icing & decoration

Using a fork, mix together the egg white, icing sugar and lemon juice in a bowl. When the icing is smooth, add the blue food colouring (spirulina will give a wonderful blue). Spread the icing on each donut, and let it dry for 1 hour. Decorate to make the donuts absolutely cosmic.

Unicorn selfie biscuits

Preparation time: 30 minutes – Cooking time: 8 minutes – Resting time: 1 hour

Makes about 30 biscuits

230 g softened butter
200 g caster sugar
1 egg
Vanilla flavour
375 g plain (all-purpose) flour
5 g baking powder
Glitter or gold gel
Black icing pen

Icing
1 egg white
2 teaspoons lemon juice
250 g icing sugar
Natural food colourings

Beat the softened butter and sugar together using a beater. Add the egg and the vanilla. Stir in the flour and baking powder mixture. Shape the dough into a ball (add some flour if it is too sticky). Wrap in plastic wrap and set aside in the refrigerator for at least 1 hour.

Preheat the oven to 180°C.

Roll out the cold dough to a thickness of around ½ cm. Cut unicorn, cloud or star shapes out of the dough using a cookie cutter. Place the biscuits on a baking tray lined with baking paper. Place the tray in the refrigerator for a few minutes before baking for 8 minutes. Take out of the oven and cool.

Icing & decoration
Mix the egg white, lemon juice and icing sugar together. The icing should be a little thick to start with, so that it stays within the shapes. Adjust the consistency by adding more icing sugar or water.

Divide into as many bowls as you have colours (remembering to leave one as white), then add the colourings to each bowl.

Ice the shapes. To make the unicorn's mane, pipe lines of different colours. Let the icing dry for a few minutes after each line. You can add a little water (very little at a time) to make the icing more liquid if it dries too quickly. Let it dry for at least 1 hour.

Decorate the horn of the unicorn with glitter or gold gel and draw in the eyes with the icing pen.

Unicom poop

Preparation time: 15 minutes – Cooking time: 1 hour

Makes about 20 unicorn droppings

60 g egg whites (2 eggs)
120 g fine caster sugar
Natural pink, green and blue
food colouring

Preheat the oven to 100°C.

Beat the egg whites to stiff peaks. At the moment they start to thicken, add the caster sugar while continuing to beat.

Divide the mixture between four bowls. Leave one bowl white and add drops of colouring to the remaining three bowls.

Lay a rectangle of plastic wrap on a flat surface. Place half the contents of one bowl into a piping bag without a nozzle. Pipe the mixture in a line on the plastic wrap. Using half the mixture from another bowl, pipe another line next to the first. Repeat this process until you have used all the mixture and have eight lines of alternating colours. Roll the plastic wrap onto itself without closing the ends and place it in a piping bag with a star nozzle.

Pipe the meringues onto a baking tray covered with a sheet of baking paper, spacing them well apart.

Bake for 1 hour at 100°C.

When they come out of the oven, place the meringues on a rack to cool, and enjoy.

The meringues will keep in an airtight container for up to 1 week.

Unicorn slice

Preparation time: 30 minutes – Cooking time: 25 to 30 minutes – Resting time: 1 hour

Makes one 40 x 35 cm tray (for about 10 people)

150 g softened butter
200 g caster sugar
1 pinch salt
3 eggs
½ teaspoon liquid or powdered vanilla extract
300 g plain (all-purpose) flour
40 g coloured sugar decorations – sprinkles (sugar strands), hundreds and thousands, stars, etc.

Frosting
40 g softened butter
110 g cream cheese
50 g icing sugar
1 to 2 teaspoons natural blue food colouring

Start by making the frosting. Beat the butter until creamy, then add the cream cheese until the mixture is well combined. Add the icing sugar and food colouring and beat the mixture until smooth.

Place this mixture into a piping bag fitted with a star or plain nozzle. Place the bag in the refrigerator for 1 hour.

Preheat the oven to 180°C.

Beat the butter with the sugar and salt to make the batter. Add the eggs, one at a time, then the vanilla. Beat continuously, then add the flour. Beat until the mixture is smooth.

Add most of the sugar decorations and mix through with a spatula. The batter should be quite thick and full of decorations. Spread this batter in a swiss roll tin to a thickness of 1 cm. Bake for 25–30 minutes.

When it comes out of the oven, let the slice cool on a rack. Once it has completely cooled, pipe small spirals of frosting on top, 2 or 3 cm in diameter, and sprinkle with the remaining sugar decorations.

Cut the slice into small squares to serve.

Unicorn cheesecake

Preparation time: 30 minutes – Refrigeration: 1 day – Resting time: 1 hour

Serves 6

200 g plain sweet biscuits
or speculaas
90 g butter
300 g Greek-style yoghurt or
fromage blanc
600 g cream cheese
1 tablespoon lemon juice
125 ml water
75 g caster sugar
2 gelatine sheets
3 or 4 different natural food
colourings

Crush the biscuits in a sealed freezer bag using a rolling pin.

Melt the butter in a microwave oven. Pour the melted butter over the crushed biscuits and work together to form a grainy dough. Use it to line the bottom of a 24–26 cm spring-form cake tin, pushing it up the sides a little by pressing a glass around the edge. Set aside in the refrigerator for 1 hour.

Mix the yoghurt with the cream cheese and lemon juice. Beat with a whisk for 2 minutes.

Boil the water in a saucepan with the caster sugar to make a syrup. Once dissolved, turn off the heat and add the gelatine, rehydrated in water beforehand. Mix well so that the gelatine completely dissolves. Pour into the yoghurt and cream cheese mix and whisk well so the mixture is combined.

Divide the mixture between three or four bowls. Add a food colouring to each bowl and mix to make pastel shades.

Remove the cheesecake base from the refrigerator and add the coloured fillings to the tin. Place one colour on top of another until all the filling is used.

Trace spirals through the filling with a wooden skewer and place in the refrigerator for 24 hours. Unmould and serve immediately.

Swiss roll

Preparation time: 25 minutes – Cooking time: 10 minutes – Resting time: 10 to 30 minutes

Serves 10

Sponge cake
4 eggs
125 g sugar
1 teaspoon vanilla extract
125 g plain (all-purpose) flour

Filling
150 g cream cheese
300 g mascarpone cheese
60 g icing sugar
Juice of 1 lemon
1 teaspoon natural blue food colouring (such as blue spirulina or klamath)
100 g small, round strawberries
Sparkly sugar decorations in blue, pink, purple, etc.

Place a sheet of baking paper on a baking tray. Oil lightly. Preheat the oven to 180°C.

Separate the eggs. Beat the egg yolks with the sugar and vanilla in a mixing bowl until pale and fluffy. Set aside.

In a second mixing bowl, beat the egg whites to stiff peaks. Fold some of the whites into the egg-yolk mixture and whisk to loosen the mixture. Fold in the rest of the whites. Add the flour in two stages and mix.

Once the mixture is combined, pour onto the baking tray. Spread out with a spatula and bake for 10 minutes.

Turn over onto a clean, damp tea towel. Lift up the tray, then remove the baking paper. Trim around the cake so the edges are sharp. Roll it up carefully in the damp tea towel. Let it rest for 10–30 minutes.

Prepare the filling by mixing the cream cheese with the mascarpone, icing sugar and lemon juice. Add the food colouring and mix in.

Unroll the sponge cake and spread it with the blue filling, then scatter with slices of strawberry. Roll up the cake again with the help of the damp tea towel. Spread the rest of the filling over the whole surface of the swiss roll. Decorate with sparkly sugar decorations. Serve immediately or place in the refrigerator.

Rainbow tiramisu

Preparation time: 35 minutes – Resting time: 1 night (at least 4 hours)

Makes 6 tiramisus

3 eggs
80 g icing sugar
1 teaspoon vanilla extract
250 g mascarpone cheese
1 pinch salt
100 g frozen raspberries
50 ml water
150 g pink sponge finger biscuits
Fondant icing in different colours
for the horn
Chantilly cream, for decorating
Sugar decorations: purple, pink,
blue and green edible glitter

Separate the eggs. Beat the sugar, egg yolks and vanilla in a mixing bowl with an electric beater until creamy. Add the mascarpone and beat again until smooth.

Beat the egg whites with a pinch of salt. When they form firm peaks, fold them gently into the mascarpone cream with a spatula.

Blend the frozen raspberries with a little water in a blender to make a coulis. Cut the pink sponge finger biscuits in half and dip them in the raspberry coulis.

Place the biscuits in six tall glasses, drizzle with coulis (1–2 tablespoons), then add some mascarpone cream. Repeat the coulis and mascarpone layers.

Place the glasses in the refrigerator overnight (or for at least 4 hours).

To make the sugar horns, roll out balls of fondant icing to make small sausages. Taking two sausages of different colours, wind them around a small wooden skewer. Place the horns in the refrigerator.

At serving time, top with whipped cream and glitter. Plant a sugar horn on top and serve.

You can also brush some gold glitter mixed with a little water onto the horns.

Unicorn cake

Preparation time: 3 hours – Cooking time: 15 minutes – Resting time: 30 minutes

Serves 6 to 8

Lime sponge cake
5 eggs
155 g sugar
1 teaspoon vanilla extract
155 g plain (all-purpose) flour
Zest of 1 lime

Swiss meringue butter cream
5 egg whites
250 g caster sugar
190 g softened butter

Assembly
Black and white fondant icing
100 g fresh raspberries
Natural food colouring (yellow, green, blue and pink)
Glitter or gold hundreds and thousands for decoration

Preheat the oven to 180°C. Butter and flour four small round cake tins, 16 cm in diameter.

Separate the eggs. Beat the egg yolks with the sugar and vanilla in a large bowl until pale and fluffy. Beat the egg whites to soft peaks in a separate bowl. Whisk some of the whites into the first mixture, then gently fold in the rest with a soft spatula. Add the flour and whisk again. Add the lime zest.

Divide the mixture evenly between the cake tins. Smooth the tops with the soft spatula. Bake the cakes for about 10 minutes. They should be lightly golden, but not brown.

Let them cool in the tin for a few minutes, then turn out the cakes while they are still quite hot. Let them cool on a rack in a single layer.

Make the swiss meringue. Heat the egg whites and caster sugar in a metal bowl over a saucepan of simmering water, beating with an electric beater on medium speed. Increase the speed gradually, until the mixture reaches approximately 50°C.

Pour the mixture into another bowl, off the saucepan, and continue to beat until completely cooled. The meringue must be smooth, supple and shiny.

Recipe continued overleaf

Unicorn cake

Take ⅔ of this mixture and incorporate the softened butter while continuing to beat for 3 minutes. The texture should be firm and creamy. Set aside the swiss meringue butter cream in the refrigerator for 30 minutes. Also set aside the remaining ⅓ of the swiss meringue in the refrigerator, to make the mane later.

Make the eyes, ears and the horn of the unicorn out of the fondant icing.

Start assembling the cake. Spread a layer of butter cream over a first round of cake, arrange a few raspberries on top, top with a second round of cake and press down lightly. Repeat the process and finish with the last cake round.

Next, cover the whole cake with a first layer of butter cream and set it aside in the refrigerator for about 10–15 minutes. Cover with a second layer of butter cream and smooth the surface. The cake must be very even. If needed, refrigerate for 10 minutes and cover with a final layer of butter cream.

Take out the remaining swiss meringue that was set aside for the mane. Divide between 5 bowls, leave one white and colour the others with yellow, green, blue and pink colouring, whisking in each colour well.

Make 5 strips of colour side by side on a piece of plastic wrap, roll up and place inside a piping bag with your choice of nozzle. (See more detailed instructions on page 32.) Set aside in the refrigerator.

Plant the horn and ears on top of the cake, then pipe the rainbow meringue all around the horn and ears, making a mane that goes down the back of the cake and comes back around the side. Arrange the eyes on the side. Sprinkle with glitter or gold hundreds and thousands.

Supernova popcorn

Preparation time: 20 minutes – Cooking time: 20 minutes

Serves 4

2 tablespoons grapeseed or sunflower oil
150 g popping corn
125 g water
125 g caster sugar
60 g unsalted butter
Natural food colouring (pink, blue and green)

Heat the oil for 2 minutes in a large saucepan then add the popping corn. Cover on a low heat and let the kernels pop for about 5 minutes, stirring from time to time.

Bring the water and sugar to the boil in a small saucepan. When a syrup has formed, add the butter. Lower the heat and cook for 5 minutes, mixing well.

Pour the syrup into three small bowls. Add a few drops of food colouring to each bowl and mix in. Add popcorn to each bowl to colour it.

Let the popcorn dry at room temperature for a few hours in a dry place, or place the bowls in the oven for 5 minutes at 160°C to dry the popcorn more quickly.

Unicorn macarons

Preparation time: 30 minutes – Cooking time: 15 minutes –
Resting time: 1 hour 30 minutes – Refrigeration time: 1 night

Makes 20 macarons

140 g egg whites (4 eggs)
185 g sugar
160 g extra fine ground almonds
(specially for macarons)
160 g icing sugar, sifted
Vanilla flavour
Your choice of flavouring
(strawberry, rosewater, violet, etc.)
Natural powdered food colourings
(do not use liquid colourings)
150 g blue melts
50 g white chocolate melts
100 ml pouring cream
1 teaspoon liquid vanilla extract
Gold food paint (or gold glitter
mixed with water)
Fondant icing for the horn (two
colours)

Use an electric beater to beat the egg whites, then add half the sugar. Continue beating until peaks form, then add the remaining sugar, increasing the speed. Whisk until all of the sugar is dissolved.

Sift the ground almonds and icing sugar into a mixing bowl and fold them gently into the beaten egg whites. Add the vanilla and chosen flavouring.

Separate the mixture into two or three bowls, depending on the number of colours you want. Add one teaspoon of food colouring to each bowl. Preheat the oven to 150°C.

Place spoonfuls of the coloured mixtures on top of each other in a piping bag. Pipe the macarons onto a sheet of baking paper on a baking tray. Pipe small, uniform rounds. Let them stand for 1 hour in a very dry place. A crust will form on the macarons.

Bake the tray of macarons for 15 minutes. Remove from the oven and allow to cool.

Melt the blue and white chocolate melts in a double boiler and mix with a spatula until smooth. Bring the pouring cream to the boil with the vanilla and pour it over the chocolate. Mix until smooth with a spatula.

Place the ganache in the refrigerator for 30 minutes. Pipe the filling on the macaron shells using a plain nozzle and top with another shell. Dab a little gold paint onto each macaron and insert a horn made out of fondant icing in the side.

Unicorn white chocolate bars

Preparation time: 10 minutes – Cooking time: 5 minutes – Resting time: 1 night

 ### Makes 4 bars

400 g white chocolate melts
180 g blue, pink or purple melts
30 g multicoloured sugar decorations
4 plastic chocolate bar moulds

Melt the white chocolate and coloured melts separately in a double boiler. Drizzle spirals of the coloured melts from a spoon into the bottom of the chocolate bar moulds and sprinkle with decorations. Pour the white chocolate over the top. Place in the refrigerator overnight.

Unmould the chocolate bars and sprinkle again with multicoloured decorations.

Enjoy with a hot white chocolate (recipe page 68).

Unicorn ice cream

Preparation time: 20 min – Freezing time : 1 night

Makes a 1-litre container of ice cream

1 litre pouring cream
3 drops vanilla extract or
1 bourbon vanilla bean
200 g sweetened condensed milk
Natural blue, pink, yellow, purple
and green food colouring.
Multicoloured sugar decorations

Beat the pouring cream with the vanilla in a large mixing bowl. When the whipped cream is firm, add the condensed milk and beat again.

Divide this mixture into five small individual bowls. Add a few drops of food colouring to each bowl and gently mix in until you have the colour you want.

Pour the contents of the five bowls one by one into an ice cream tray, so the colours are on top of each other. Trace figure eights with a wooden skewer to mix the colours. Sprinkle with decorations and place the tray in the freezer overnight.

The next day, take the tray out 15 minutes before scooping the ice cream.

54

Coloured smoothie popsicles

Preparation time: 20 minutes – Freezing time: at least 1 night

Makes 10 popsicles

Blueberries
Strawberries
Blackberries
Mango
Passionfruit
Dragon fruit
800 g plain yoghurt
80 g sugar or agave syrup
A few drops natural food colourings or blue spirulina
1 silicone popsicle mould with 10 wooden popsicle sticks

Cut the fruit into slices or pieces and divide them between bowls according to colour. Set a few slices of fruit aside for decoration.

Add the sugar or syrup to the yoghurt. Leave half the yoghurt plain and mix the remainder with the food colourings to create several different colours.

Place the pieces of fruit in the bottom of the moulds, then pour in a little plain yoghurt. Finish filling the popsicle moulds with different colours of yoghurt. Each popsicle should have its own colour.

Place in the freezer for at least one night.

Gently unmould and enjoy straight away!

Unicorn frozen yoghurt bites

Preparation time: 10 minutes – Freezing time: 1 night (at least 4 hours)

Serves 4

1 silicone tray with heart- or star-shaped holes (or an ice cube tray)
300 g Greek-style yoghurt
30 g sugar or runny honey
2 teaspoons liquid or powdered vanilla extract
Your choice of natural food colourings (at least three)
Some strips of rainbow candy

Whisk the yoghurt with the sugar and vanilla. Divide the mixture between as many bowls as you would like colours.

Add the colourings to each bowl, then mix in until you have the colour you want.

Fill a piping bag without a nozzle with tablespoons of yoghurt in each colour, layering on top of one other. Fill the holes in the tray. The colours will mix.

Place the bites in the freezer overnight.

Unmould the bites and top each with a piece of rainbow candy to decorate.

Starlight smoothie bowl

Preparation time: 15 minutes

Makes 2 bowls

150 ml almond milk
100 ml coconut milk
125 g plain or vanilla yoghurt
1 banana
50 g blueberries
2 tablespoons agave syrup
Natural blue food colouring
1 handful blackberries
2 tablespoons frozen raspberries
A few coconut flakes
½ kiwifruit
3 slices dragon fruit
Gold edible glitter

Pour the almond milk, coconut milk and yoghurt into a blender. Add the banana, sliced into rounds, blueberries (set a few aside for decoration), agave syrup and the blue food colouring. Blend until you get a nice blue and creamy smoothie.

Pour into two bowls, then decorate with the remaining blueberries, blackberries, crumbled frozen raspberries, coconut flakes, and kiwifruit and dragon fruit cut into stars with a cookie cutter.

Sprinkle with gold glitter and serve immediately.

You can add other super foods to this smoothie, such as acai, maca powder or hulled hemp seeds.

Blue latté

Preparation time: 5 minutes – Cooking time: 1 minute

Makes 2 glasses

200 ml almond, oat or rice milk
50 ml coconut milk
1 teaspoon ground ginger
Juice of ½ lemon
2 teaspoons agave syrup
Natural blue food colouring (or blue spirulina or klamath powder)
Edible glitter, to decorate

Blend all the ingredients except the glitter in a blender, then heat them in the microwave or serve cold.

Pour into glasses or mugs.

Sprinkle with glitter.

Banana raspberry frappé

Preparation time: 15 minutes

Makes 2 glasses

Blue coulis
60 g white chocolate melts
2 tablespoons coconut cream
A few drops natural blue food colouring (or use melts that are already coloured)

Pink smoothie
100 ml almond milk or reduced-fat milk
2 bananas, sliced into rounds and frozen
100 g frozen raspberries
1 tablespoon grenadine or strawberry syrup
½ dragon fruit
4 tablespoons whipped coconut cream
Pink and blue edible decorations

For the blue coulis, melt the white chocolate in a double boiler, then add the coconut cream and mix to a smooth and creamy coulis. Add the blue food colouring and mix again. Set aside.

For the pink smoothie, blend the almond milk with the frozen bananas and raspberries in a blender. Add the grenadine or syrup and the dragon fruit cut into chunks and blend again. Adjust the consistency: add almond milk or water if the smoothie is too thick to be drunk through a straw.

Make spirals of blue chocolate coulis around the sides of two tall glasses and pour in the pink smoothie. Top with whipped cream and decorate. Serve immediately.

You can also top with some raspberry coulis or more blue coulis.

Rainbow smoothies

Preparation time: 20 minutes

Makes 2 large glasses or jars

5 strawberries
3 bananas
A few raspberries
50 g other berries
50 g blueberries or blackberries
(or acai powder)
1 kiwifruit
½ mango
100 ml pineapple juice
250 g Greek-style yoghurt
½ dragon fruit
Edible decorations

The day before, cut up and freeze all the fruits in plastic bags (or use already frozen fruits).

At serving time, blend the strawberries, 2 tablespoons of banana, 2 tablespoons of pineapple juice and 2 tablespoons Greek yoghurt in a blender, then pour into a large glass or jar. Repeat the process with the same quantity of banana, yoghurt and pineapple juice, each time adding, in turn, the frozen raspberries and other berries, blueberries, kiwifruit and the mango, to make several layers of colour.

Finish by decorating the smoothie, adding a pretty straw and a slice of dragon fruit cut into a star, or a few blueberries.

Serve immediately or screw on the lid of the jar to take to the office or a picnic.

Galaxy mocktails

Preparation time: 5 minutes – Freezing time: 6 hours

Makes 4 cocktails

1 litre bottle of lemonade
50 ml grenadine syrup
2 limes
A few drops blue food colouring
4 cocktail cherries
Purple sugar

Pour half the bottle of lemonade into an ice cream tray or baking tin. Place in the freezer for 3 hours, then scrape with a fork to make crystals. Return to the freezer for 3 hours and scrape the granita again. If it is still not frozen enough, place in the freezer for another hour.

Pour a measure of grenadine into each glass. Fill to the rim with granita. Slice the limes into rounds. Place them against the sides of each glass. Pour in the rest of the lemonade, then a few drops of food colouring. Add a cherry. Sprinkle with purple sugar.

Serve immediately!

Unicorn hot white chocolate

Preparation time: 10 minutes – Cooking time: 5 minutes

Makes 2 cups

100 g white chocolate melts
A few drops natural pink food colouring (or use melts that are already coloured)
250 ml full-cream or reduced-fat milk
1 tablespoon liquid vanilla extract or a tablespoon grenadine syrup
Whipped cream
A few mini-marshmallows

Horns
50 g white chocolate for melting
Natural blue food colouring
2 ice cream cones
Edible glitter

For the horns, melt a few white chocolate melts with some blue food colouring in a double boiler, mixing together well. Cut 5 cm off the top of the cones to make mini-horns. Dip them quickly in the melted blue chocolate, then in the glitter. Place in the freezer for 1 hour.

For the hot chocolate, melt the white chocolate melts in the double boiler with the pink food colouring, mixing well.

Heat the milk in a saucepan, then pour it over the melted pink chocolate in the double boiler. Beat with a hand whisk. Add the vanilla or syrup and mix again. The hot chocolate should be very smooth and creamy.

Pour the hot chocolate into cups and top with whipped cream. Sprinkle with mini-marshmallows and top with the unicorn horns.

Serve immediately.

Unicorn milkshakes

Preparation time: 15 minutes

Makes 2 large glasses

250 ml reduced-fat milk
500 g vanilla ice cream
Natural pink, blue, yellow, purple
and green food colouring
A few marshmallows to decorate
A few sugar decorations – sprinkles
(sugar strands), multicoloured
hundreds and thousands, etc.

Blend the cold milk with the ice cream in a blender
for 30 seconds.

Pour the mixture into five bowls and add a different
food colouring to each bowl. Mix quickly with a
whisk or fork. Pour a little of each colour into tall
glasses. The colours will mix and form a rainbow.

Serve immediately with the marshmallows,
multicoloured decorations and gold straws.

Acknowledgements

I would especially like to thank Juliette Garnier for her talent, accuracy and help with making the recipes.

I would also like to thank Jennifer for helping me to find, from the other side of the Atlantic, very 'unicorn' ideas and products.

Thanks to Olivier for his daily company, support and talent as a retoucher!

Thanks to Marabout and Claudie Souchet for their support and enthusiasm for this wonderful project.

To help you with decorations and to make beautiful colours, here are some essential sites:

– www.fancysprinkles.com

– www.scrapcooking.fr/en

– www.essentialingredient.com.au

– www.cakerswarehouse.com.au

Published in 2017 by Murdoch Books, an imprint of Allen & Unwin
First published by Hachette Livre (Marabout) in 2017

Murdoch Books Australia
83 Alexander Street
Crows Nest NSW 2065
Phone: +61 (0) 2 8425 0100
Fax: +61 (0) 2 9906 2218
murdochbooks.com.au
info@murdochbooks.com.au

Murdoch Books UK
Ormond House
26–27 Boswell Street
London WC1N 3JZ
Phone: +44 (0) 20 8785 5995
murdochbooks.co.uk
info@murdochbooks.co.uk

For Corporate Orders & Custom Publishing, contact our Business Development Team at salesenquiries@murdochbooks.com.au

Publisher: Corinne Roberts
Designer: David Robayo – 34 studio
Translator: Melissa McMahon
Production: Lou Playfair

© Hachette Livre (Marabout) 2017

A cataloguing-in-publication entry is available from the catalogue of the National Library of Australia at nla.gov.au.

ISBN 978 1 76063 195 6 Australia
ISBN 978 1 76063 4414 UK

A catalogue record for this book is available from the British Library.

Colour reproduction by Splitting Image Colour Studio Pty Ltd, Clayton, Victoria

Printed by Graficas Estella, Spain